Treasures of Life

A BOOK OF POETRY

Linda Lee Morley

Treasures of Life: A Book of Poetry

Copyright © 2023 Linda Lee Morley. All rights reserved. No part of this book may be reproduced or retransmitted in any form or by any means without the written permission of the publisher.

Published by Wheatmark®
2030 East Speedway Boulevard, Suite 106
Tucson, Arizona 85719 USA
www.wheatmark.com

ISBN: 979-8-88747-012-2 (paperback)
ISBN: 979-8-88747-013-9 (ebook)
LCCN: 2022920753

Bulk ordering discounts are available through Wheatmark, Inc.
For more information, email orders@wheatmark.com or call 1-888-934-0888.

Contents

A Babbling Book of Poetry ix

LOVE

Cost of Kindness 3

Can I Love That Way Again? 4

A Lost Spark 5

Happy Father's Day 6

When I'm With You 7

Abundant Love 8

Too Smart to Let You Go 10

Passion 11

I Miss You 13

The Secret to a Successful Marriage 14

My Eighth-Grade Love 15

On Our Wedding Night 16

I'll Get By Beautifully 17

FAITH

Faith 21

Final Flight 22

A Good Foundation 23

Widowed 24

Love Is the Key 25

God Loves Me Any Way 26

Happiness Is Not a Thing 28

God Had a Blessing 29

God Is There! 30

Give God a Chance 33

Slow Me Down Lord 34

Songs to Reach the Son 35

God Knows! 36

Grandma's Mansion 37

There Is a Plan for You and I 38

Triumph in the Dawn 39

The Other Side of Today 40

The Job Hunter's Prayer 41

Lead Me 42

Wonder 43

TRIALS

Trials 47

Do You Ever Wonder Why? 48

When Love Goes 48

Don't Grieve for Me 49

Divorced 51

Don't Cry for Me 53

Lost Love 54

The Quick Tongue of a Fool. 56

Diet Help 57

She Didn't Cry. 58

Someone Who Likes Who I Am 60

Were You There? 61

Words 62

Youth Regained? 63

Tears. 64

An Old Man 65

THOUGHTS

A Merry-Go-Round of Misery. 69

Decisions 71

Bye 72

Clouds. 73

Peace 74

Love 75

Mountain Man 76

Sunscreen 77

Tidbits. 78

Picking up the Pieces. 79

Think Thin 80

Take Five. 81

Free Will 83

My Soul Longs for the Seasons of My Youth 85

Oh Lord, Won't You Bring Me! 86

Why Did I Buy the Air Fryer? 87

When the Quarantine Is Over 88

GROWTH

Forbidden Fruit 91

Choose 94

If Only 96

It's Your Mood, Control It! 98

Twentieth Class Reunion 100

Put Yourself in His Place 101

Inheritance Now? 103

No Good Looking Back 105

Not That Hard to Love 106

About That Job 107

Staying Single 112

Brand New Start 114

The Mistake 115

Abortion 116

An Unanswered Question 118

Feel Your Grief 120

Lessons 122

Love Outgrown 123

Goodbye 124

Resolve 125

Wishing Won't Do 126

Believe in Yourself 127

A Babbling Book of Poetry

I have a book of poetry

Bubbling up inside of me

I've written many lines of verse

At times it even seems a curse

For poetry creeps up on me

In every desk or book I see

I've stashed my lines of constant rhymes

Inside of everything I find

So if I could compile a book

I could unearth my babbling brook

LOVE

Cost of Kindness

No matter what your parents said or what you do believe,
No wedding ring can hold someone who truly wants to leave.

So treat your partner justly, and spend some time with them.
For they have expectations too, are you up to them?

Don't take their love for granted, nothing good was ever free.
And if you want their love for life, a cost there has to be.

You'll have to give a little and bend a bit or two.
For when they need attention, you'll have to give that too.

For most of us need someone. It seems vital to our needs.
But living with somebody else must take a special breed.

A breed that knows this closeness will have its own rewards.
This simple cost of kindness every couple can afford.

Can I Love That Way Again?

Will I just keep on searching for someone to take his place?

Or is it really hopeless that I'd match his warm embrace?

Sometimes when I think back upon the love I felt for him

Deep down inside I wonder can I love that way again?

Will I miss those laughing eyes of his, the way he smiled and talked,

Our conversations over coffee and so many afternoon walks?

No one in my life made me laugh the way he did,

He had that special something, made me feel just like a kid.

I looked so pretty through his eyes, no one else saw me that way.

That perfect place inside his love was where I longed to stay.

A love so deep that even now thinking back brings back the tears.

I still recall the love I felt and will for many years.

A Lost Spark

As we date each other it isn't hard to see

    You're really not a prince at all high upon a steed

Time has passed and you have changed, your smile seems to have gone

    You're not the one I once loved—no, something's very wrong

And as I try so hard to find the love that we once knew

    It's clear that only memories remain of our love tune

I try in vane to find a spark of the love we used to share

    Only memories are remaining of how much you cared

You don't spark the flame in me and I don't see you stir

    Let's say goodbye so we can save the memories that endure.

Happy Father's Day

For all the times I used your tools and never put them back

    For all the times I took the car and never thought to ask

For all your paints I used up doing work for someone else

    I never once replaced your stuff, my thoughts were of myself

I was always in a rush and never gave a thought to you

    Till I'd get myself in trouble then I'd ask you what to do

You were there when I needed you, it seems I took you for granted

    It's just so hard to tell you, Dad, you're the best Dad on the planet

When I'm With You

I love the way you make me feel so pretty.
    No one else has made me feel so happy.
I love the way you make me laugh,
    How time with you goes by so fast.
I love the way we giggle when we're together,
    In sunny, or in cold and stormy weather.
When I'm with you all I ever do is sing.
    It hardly matters what other people think.
I forget my troubles when we're together
    When I'm with you that's all that really matters.
When I'm with you I feel that I am someone.
    It doesn't matter that no one else does.
I feel so much acceptance and I can grow here.
    Knowing that you love me as I am, dear.
We've been in love so many years, my darling.
    We have four kids and we know it wasn't easy.
You're black and I am white, but does it matter?
    I'd rather die if we couldn't be together.

Abundant Love

He held me when I needed love, his tenderness was mine
He loved me in a special way I grew to feel so fine
He made me feel so elegant like I could do no wrong
In everything I wanted, he'd always go along

I do suppose he spoiled me, that was something very new
He loved the way I giggled and the silly things I'd do
I seemed to feel much better about everything I did
No more self-consciousness, no feelings to keep hid

This was a new sensation this acceptance that I felt
I'd always been self-conscious, quite afraid to be myself
His love had brought excitement and new feelings of great joy
Even though it turned out he had used me like a toy

The hurt I felt tore through me and it brought me to my knees
It made me look to Heaven as I cried out "Help me please"
God was there to pick me up when I had fallen down
God had been there all the time patiently waiting around

God knew someday I'd call on Him to help me with my life
God knew someday I'd realize His love could conquer strife
God would never desert me His love was greater than
Any love and acceptance I could get from any man

God's supply of love is endless and far greater than we know
God was waiting for my call so He'd have a chance to show
All the wonders that God offers and the miracles He will do
God loves everything about us, there's love enough for me and you

If a mortal could accept me and love me openly
Make me feel so confident it was just okay to be me
Think how much you love somebody, God loves you even more
God's love is so abundant now who could ask for more?

Too Smart to Let You Go

You said my love that I was not to tell you I love you

    I'm not to say those little words though I know they are true

I guess I'll have to make the most of other words I know

    To tell you that I care so much and want to make it show

I do adore those eyes of yours, blue as the sky above

    When you take me in your arms, it's all that I dream of

I never wanted money, for the rich have problems too

    I only want to hold you and to be there next to you

I may have never told you what a handsome man you are

    How finding you has made me the richest girl by far

I will not say I love you since to please you I'll refrain

    I'll only say that I'll be there through snow, sleet, and rain

So many times you've hurt inside over stupid girls you know

    Your hurting days are over, I'm too smart to let you go

Passion

I'd love to share your dreams with you

    If only it could be

I'd love to share my dreams with you

    Come lie and dream with me

Let's lie and dream a little while

    And leave the world behind

Let's be somewhere among the clouds

    And watch the world go by

So let me share my dreams with you

    Imagine if you can

Day in and out we'd love and live

    Inside my fairy land

I'll make your cares and worries, Dear

    All vanish in the night

I promise they will not return
       Until I'm out of sight

So dream with me my gorgeous love
       And know this to be true

My life could never be the same
       Now that I have known you

I Miss You

Isn't it just the most absurd notion that you ever heard?

I can be working at my job and find myself choked by a sob.

I'll think of you though you've been gone so many years it seems

You're in my life and wake me up so often in my dreams

Though we divorced long before you died it really matters not

I loved you oh so very much and can forget you not

The Secret to a Successful Marriage

When you believe in God above
And ask the Lord to send you love.
When God tells you the choice He made
By chasing other loves away.
When then you take those wedding vows
You know God's choice has been involved.
When doubts pop up, put them aside
God made the choice you must abide.
The secret is you've chose a mate
There's only one, don't contemplate.
The trials that in your life there'll be
Will smooth out if they don't rile thee.
And should you long for days of old
For other loves you wish to hold
You know God meant your spouse for thee
Keep all the doubts from spreading seed.
If being single was such delight
Why did you long for a wedding night?
Should you divorce, you'd marry again
That's when real troubles begin!

My Eighth-Grade Love

We look for love around the clock, we hope each day to find
One extra special person that we'd like to share our time.
I've searched two thousand days and more to find Prince Charming true.
And just to think that long ago I knew him and he was you.
A man of men, for you were there to share the special times.
The times we hid inside the gym and held our passion in line.
Yes you were there to share my hurts and every joy I knew.
You treated me with velvet glove, tender and generous too.
And through the years I lost my way, I stumbled looking on
To what I thought I wanted, for excitement, I wandered on.
I wandered through the high school years and saw not what was there.
I didn't see your qualities or notice if you cared.
I wonder if I'd have the chance to find you ever again.
To find the arms that held me, that sheltered me within.
Could I have a chance to know you like I knew you once before?
Can I share the laughter with you like the days I did adore?
I'd feel I was the luckiest girl there was in all the world.
If you could care for me again and set my heart awhirl.

On Our Wedding Night

If I could make the world stand still
then this is where I'd be.
And we could stay here in this room
for all eternity.
Then we could stay here in this bed
and let all time pass by.
For there's no better spot on earth
then right here at your side.
For loving you brings me great joy
it's lasted for some while.
I am aware there's no better view
then watching my man smile.
And you my man you make me proud,
so proud to be with you.
To show you off to all the world will
make my dreams come true.
For in the world of men and mayhem
a twosome we will be.
Because my man, my man of men,
you now belong to me.

I'll Get By Beautifully

I do not search for riches or a fancy car to drive.
    Fashions of the latest style won't make me satisfied.
When I went to high school, I was certain of one thing.
    A partner to share my life with, my happiness would bring.
A lovely house with everything could burn up over night.
    The most precious jewelry could be taken from my sight.
All these worldly symbols of status and affluence
    wouldn't hold me when I was lonely or help me when I was depressed.

Someone to share the quiet times like coffee time with me.
    Someone who understood my moods and liked my company.
Someone who's not impressed by looks, make-up, and fancy clothes.
    I felt someone to count on was more precious than those.
I searched through bars and nightclubs but only found drunks there.
    In fancy spots I soon found out so few people really care.
All I could find was misery, pain killers in bottles and jars.
    People spend lots of money to escape their fears and scars.

There are so many users out there looking for a score.
    It made me want to hide from life, locked up inside my door.
Good people with their heads on straight have little time for booze.
    They know the next morning they'll wake sick and confused.
A person should save their money, put their trust in God and find,
    that a decent person to share their life will come to them in time.
I know that I'll meet someone at church, recreation, or at work.
    Who, like me, sees the cop-outs others try that just don't work.

I know that God's good to everyone and He will show the way
    for anyone to find someone who we can share our day.
God will also show us how to find a way to live
    without the silly thrills that Satan wants to give.
With God as my life partner I'll find happiness amid strife
    He'll show me the direction He intended for my life.
I cried so much for someone's love and through the tears I cried
    I found I wouldn't gain a thing till I gave up my pride.

I know I'll have the right someone when God's time is right.
    You'll lead me to the perfect job, Your plan is always right.
Help me to draw closer Lord, I want to be with You
    Help me to be the person who will draw others to You.
I know I have Your guidance every step along the way.
    Each and every tomorrow brings a bright and shiny day.
I'll get by, Lord, beautifully, because You're here with me.
    There just aren't any problems that You can't solve for me.

FAITH

Faith

The rich have problems too I've always said

Some women that I know share a bed

With someone who I wouldn't be caught dead

To keep the diamonds and the life they've led

Now I would rather have a love complete

Than all the riches dreamed of in my sleep

The love I'm speaking of comes from above

With God I found acceptance full of love

He's there no matter what I choose to do

He shares my moods and cheers me when I'm blue

I do not fear someone will steal from me

Possessions, for I don't let them own me

My greatest joy now comes from Faith not rings

Insurance costs are low on spiritual things

And should I own a diamond to admire

I still know Faith is valued even higher

Final Flight

As the body goes into its grave

And the dust takes back its own

Our soul takes flight from our body's weight

And soars to heights unknown

The closer it gets to Heaven above

Earth's encumbrances are outgrown.

If on this earth we felt God's love

We can glimpse our future home.

A Good Foundation

When I was young you made me go to church on Sunday morn

    You even had me baptized shortly after I was born

Down through the years I came to understand that God was there

    And when I got in trouble I could turn to Him in prayer

I've taught my kids to understand the significance of God

    They tell me they wouldn't give Him up, no matter what the cause

If I should change religions, they tell me they would not

    I'm glad I have God with me for I lean on Him a lot

It would be rough to raise two kids alone if I had to

    I'm glad God was beside me and told me what to do

No matter what my trials may be with God I will be strong

    Thanks Mom, for my foundation, to build my future on

Widowed

Help me find hope in this void death has made
Help me see sunshine in this cloudy day

Help me sort slowly through all of my troubles
Help me see blessings somewhere in this rubble

Lead me, Lord, guide me, then teach me to pray
Prayers that will make me turn sorrow away

I know that you love me in my hour of need
The loved one I'm missing can't be here with me

Maybe it's time I took stock in myself
No longer wishing to be someone else

I've always had someone to lean on too much
It's high time I stood up and threw off my crutch

For though I'm alone life goes on anyway
Help me find cheer as I start each new day

Help me to focus on family and friends
Help me remember on You I depend

Love Is the Key

I have seen the glory and felt the presence of the Lord

I wouldn't want to wander from the life God has in store

For peace and beauty, love and hope are waiting there for me

I only have to open up my heart, God's love is free.

For God is love and I must learn to open my heart to Him

For pure unselfish love's the key to joy and peace within

I trust in God and every day new happiness I find

I'm so very glad I found the Lord and He is mine.

God Loves Me Any Way

It isn't how many verses you can memorize for church
We shouldn't be discouraged if total recall doesn't work
It isn't very important what clothing we should wear
It's how much we love Jesus when we come to Him in prayer

It isn't just important that the Bible we've read through
God also looks at kindness and the decent things we do
Only God can understand what prompted us to try
Only God can be with us when all alone we cry

God knows the feeling in our heart and knows what keeps us home
Away from church, at home we pray 'bout burdens of our own
When I am in my closet and know only He can hear
No matter what my sins have been I know He's always near

He knows that these distractions are still fitting in His plan
God loves me even when I'm lost and I don't understand
God loves me 'cause I need Him and He patiently waits for me
When I've chosen the wrong path forgetting to follow His lead

God loves me 'cause He made me full of pride and stubbornness
God will be there when I call out "get me out of this mess"
I don't use God to fall back on when I have done my thing
He knows I must try it my way though it will probably sting

For God wants me to try it, only then can I choose
God's way over Satan's, with Satan's way I lose
God loves me and He wants me there because I want to be
God loves me cause I'm no puppet, and His I choose to be

God loves me and I love Him more when I have lost my way
Someday I'll understand it all and only go God's way
God loves me and God loves you and His love does not depend
On whether we have earned it for God loves us all, my friend

Happiness Is Not a Thing

He runs all night then sleeps all day
His weekends seem to be that way
He's searching for some happiness
That's something no one can possess
For happiness is not a thing
It's found inside your very being
It comes from doing little things
For someone that you know has needs
It doesn't come from boastful deeds
Done to serve as ego feed
It comes from an unselfish act
You could have very easily passed
Then you don't mention it again
For Jesus knows it, no more need said
For your reward is in your heart
You feel good that's the very best part
Remind yourself each and every day
You are special, God made you that way

God Had a Blessing

I asked the Lord because I was a sinner

    I needed help I hurt so deep inside

In His love I bathed and found acceptance

    I gained His strength, found wisdom on my side

God gave me hope and faith in each tomorrow

    God gave me strength to change each part of me

I began a trip to find a new awareness

    Seeing the anguish my old habits brought me

I needed to change and God was there to change me

    I saw my habits and thoughts were hurting me

My whole life had brought on my destruction

    Only God could accomplish the miracle I'd need

I didn't know the wonders God had envisioned

    I'd only asked that He would just love me

I'd asked for love but given in the bargain

    God had a blessing waiting there for me

God Is There!

Some people reach the end of their rope believing no one cares
They let go of what hope they have and drop into despair
While others reach the end of their rope refusing to give up
They tie a big knot in it and hang on looking up

For at the end of every rope there always is a choice
You look down in self-pity giving discouragement a voice
Or you can choose the higher view and look above with hope
For God is there to answer prayers at the end of every rope

God gave us each an active mind and gave each one a choice
The world around us beckons loud, God has a softer voice
We just don't want to listen, we're too busy with our lives
It's only when we mess things up that we ever realize

That God above is always there just waiting for our call
It's a shame we don't call on Him till we make a mess of it all
After we've tried it our way and found it doesn't work
After we've chased a daydream and acted like a jerk

After many years of marriage, somebody wants to leave
After a life of loving, death brings us time to grieve
After the things we've wanted bring misery and pain
When someone's neglect or greed has caused heartaches to rain

We've built our dreams on sandy ground or took too much for granted
The house would hold if on a ROCK, our hopes and dreams were planted
God is the ROCK OF AGES and His glory He has shown
He works in many special ways with purpose of his own

No matter what your dream has been God understands the hurt
God is the great physician and the healer of this earth
God can heal the broken heart, He'll heal the broken head
God heals the hearts of loved ones when the one they loved is dead

So if you're the one who's crying when you didn't have your way
Dry your tears and rest assured it's the beginning of a new day
A day when you'll see the glory and the wisdom in God's voice
The day that you will realize you've always had the choice

So choose to pull yourself up and listen to God's call
For God has the solution and the insight for us all
So make sure when your hurdles come and you're running in the heat
You've said a prayer, God will be there, there's no need He can't meet!

Everyday I thank the Lord above for heartaches that I had
That brought me crying to my knees and made me hurt so bad
The hopeless way I felt that day God came into my life
God made me realize that good comes out of pain and strife

When I cried out, "God, help, I can't take it anymore"
It seemed His peaceful presence overpowered me for sure
I stopped my tortured sobs of grief and kneeled there in the dark
I sensed that I was not alone for God entered my heart

In three hours came the dawn I got up out of bed
On my dresser glowing was a candle colored red
I could not light that candle in the storm the night before
God lit that candle and I knew I'd be alone no more!

Give God a Chance

I've heard it said God answers prayers
But sometimes the answer is no
How many times have you heard this?
How many believe that it's so?
I thought all my answers were negative
I really had given up hope
It took a long time to show me
His love had a much broader scope
Too often we give up on Jesus
Stubbornly do things our way
If only we'd waited, the perfect solution
God's answer was still on its way
God loves us and cares for us dearly
His resources are greater than ours
If we'd only trust in His positive love
We'd have waited and saved ourselves scars
Give God a chance and pray knowing
The prayer will be answered the best
If we'd only believe and give God a chance
God's love would have passed all the tests

Slow Me Down Lord

Slow me down Lord so I might do
    All the work that you want me to do

Slow me down Lord so I might see
    All the beauty you made for me.

Slow me down Lord that I might be
    The kind of Christian you want me to be.

Lord grant me patience, teach me to pray
    Teach me to love You and turn the right way.

Slow down my pace, teach me to wait
    Lord won't you teach me to love and not hate.

Slow me down Lord, teach me to see
    All your children need guidance like me.

Songs to Reach the Son

I had a dream, my children had just left me and in the dream they'd turned away and run.

I was so hurt because I so loved them. I had been there before their lives begun.

It hurts so much and seemed so real, the hurt had literally woke me up.

As I laid there in the total darkness, I thought of God who loved us all that much.

How it must hurt when we turn our lives from Him. How He cares for each and everyone.

He loves us so and He denies us nothing. He only asks for love from anyone.

The Lord's love is waiting for the asking. He has abundant love for everyone.

God rejoices when just one soul turns to Him. Angels sing their songs to reach the Son.

God Knows!

God knows how many grains of sand are lying on the beach
    God knows how many of our dreams are just within our reach

God knows the number of hairs we each have on our head
    God knows just how many words each one of us has said

God knows how many drops of water there are in each lake
    God knows how many grains of flour we put into a cake

God knows that we can't understand or see these quantities
    God knows these facts are hidden from you and from me

God knows our strengths and weaknesses the troubles we endure
    God knows of our hurt feelings, disappointments come for sure

God knows we only need to ask and He can intervene
    God knows He has to wait till then to meet our every need

God knows too just how peaceful life could be when He's the guide
    God knows the choice is left to us He waits for you and I

Grandma's Mansion

"Where did Grandma go when she died, Mommy?"
"Why won't she be home when we are visiting?"
"Is Grandma in the ground?" No, it's just her bones.
"Will she come to visit?" No, her soul went home.
"Is there a pretty place to be and can we go?"
Her home is up in heaven and someday you will go.
"Is dying very painful?" No, she died in her sleep.
Everybody dies, my child, when this life is complete.
Jesus makes a place for us in Heaven up above.
When our place is all prepared Jesus bring us up.
Every one that died before is waiting for us there.
It's such a joyful place to be, where there are no more cares.
They sing and dance and celebrate, they have so much fun.
If we could see it, we couldn't wait for this life to be done.
Now Grandma is in Heaven and Grandpa's waiting there.
They've got so much to talk about their notes to compare.
Grandma's been so lonely waiting all these years.
Her mansion's finally finished; Jesus has her near.

There Is a Plan for You and I

Jesus makes a place for you and I
A mansion of our own up in the sky
Someday when our work on earth is done
We will join Him in heaven having fun
Building a house of gold in the sky
For Jesus builds a place for you and I
Not everyone can die when they choose
Some play games of chance, and many lose
Now if you wish to waste what time you have
Not accomplishing the task God planned
A vacant tombstone's all that's left of you
God will send another your job to do
There's so little time for you to be
A shining example of creative seed
God planted in each person when born
To live triumphantly in earthly form
While we are on earth the choice is ours
To have a dream and push it to the stars
It's in God's plan, it's right for you and me
God wants the very best for us to be

Triumph in the Dawn

Lord above bring to my soul your gladness.

Teach me Lord to face each trial that comes.

Show me how to face my joy and sadness.

Knowing you're there with guidance and with love.

Hold me Lord and give my tears your comfort.

Show me Lord how I'll make it through the day.

Love me Lord now that I feel so lonely

For I know in Your arms I'll find the way.

Show me Lord the beauty in my teardrops.

Show me how to walk looking above.

Help me help my sisters and my brothers

Help me comfort others with your love.

Lead me now as I journey to tomorrow

Knowing that your love will guide me on.

I shall face the evening and its sorrows

For I know there's triumph in the dawn.

The Other Side of Today

I do believe there is a place just a breath or two away
That occupies the space I'm in on the other side of today
The place I live is only here where mortals have to dwell
If it hadn't been for Adam we might all be living well
If he wouldn't have bitten the apple on that very fateful day
We could all be there together on the other side of today
It's a beautiful Garden of Eden where everyone goes when they die
I'll find my earthly father there when this life of mine goes by
My Grandpa is patiently waiting for Grandma to join him I know
It's right here among us that heavenly land where we will surely go
Their spirits are living beside us, the loved ones who've traveled beyond
There are flowers and trees in abundance such a pleasure to look out upon
So many people fear dying afraid of a future unknown
If they only knew, it's a beautiful view that place where God's flowers are grown
Once we die to this life in this time frame we will live through eternity there
We'll have shed ourselves of these bodies and we'll gracefully float through the air
After a visit with Jesus we'll go back to that garden God made
It's a beautiful spot where we'll praise God a lot on the other side of today

The Job Hunter's Prayer

Father in heaven, help me I pray

My bank account gets smaller each day.

I know when the time's right

I'll get the right job

And that in the meantime

It won't help to sob

I know you know best

And for me in the end

You'll send me a great job

Like there's never been

I know in the past

I have counted on you

You will never fail me

You always come through

Lead Me

You've brought me so far Lord

You've showed me so much

You've brought me a long way

Toward seeing your love

As I keep on following

The path that you lead

Show me your will Lord

And take mine from me

For you are my tour guide

I'm glad of the trip

Just show me the road Lord

And don't let me slip

Wonder

Where do the raindrops come from?

Where does a dewdrop go?

Will the sun rise in the morning?

Only God the Father knows.

TRIALS

Trials

We must not fear the vast unknown

Though we can't see what lies beyond

The problems that will come our way

Are there for us to grow upon

Do You Ever Wonder Why?

You've heard about the Indian and his moccasins?

Or the song that said walk a mile in my shoes?

If we'd put ourselves in the place of those we're judging

Maybe we wouldn't be so quick to accuse?

When Love Goes

There are wounds that must be healed

As the death of love brings pain

There must be time to mourn the loss

Then it's time to love again

Don't Grieve for Me

Don't grieve for me when I have died
In death there's peace, in peace I lie
Please help the ones I leave behind
I'll wait for them on the other side

Don't lose your days in grief for me
You must learn as we part company
That life is something loaned to you
It goes back to God when you are through

So make the best of every day
And help someone along the way
There are so many chances lost
To help somebody bear their cross

In helping others in little ways
You give some meaning to your days
And when the moment comes for you
You've done the best that you can do

Too selfishly we go through life
Grabbing money and merchandise
There's so much importance given things
Our lives soon lose their real meaning

We leave our friends in search of wealth
And work so hard we lose our health
Then when death comes we long for love
Closeness to family and friends long gone

Along the way we let them go
Was money worth this dying alone?
Don't grieve for me when I am gone
Make your life one you can look back well on

Make sure each day you face with cheer
You may not have another year
There is no sadness if you realize
Life is loaned for you to utilize

Each hour of the day you're living in
Will never come your way again
Bring laughter into every day
Make others glad you came their way

Don't grieve for me, I'm out of time
The ones who hurt are left behind
I've lived life in the fullest way
Trying to help others along the way

Divorced

I know I can't explain it to the children or myself
 A part of me still loves you and really can't be helped.

I loved you, oh so very much when we were newly wed.
 Through the years it passed away, the heartaches came instead.

We just couldn't give each other the support we seemed to need.
 From all our disappointments came heartaches and such grief.

Maybe if we'd been wiser we'd have realized things were wrong.
 Maybe we'd have worked it out before it went on so long.

There must have been something missing in the way we viewed our lives.
 There had to be a reason we couldn't work out married life.

We just could not communicate or see each other's needs.
 We each sought out someone else to whom our case we'd plead.

Our marriage lacked commitment, we didn't support each other.
 Too many nights were spent alone, our careers replaced each other.

I know I just couldn't live with you if I could not be true.
I couldn't be that kind of wife, that's something I wouldn't do.

I don't think I was good for you if you had to look elsewhere.
We brought out the worst in each other, it really wasn't fair.

There're parts of you I'll always love and that won't go away.
I just had to find someone whose trust I could repay.

I do wish the best for you as you go along life's way.
I hope the kids will understand it has to be this way.

You have to be the kind of man that you have chosen too.
I know for us it can't work out no matter what we do.

I wish you lots of happiness in all the years to come.
I hope you'll be successful in the work you have begun.

Just because we're not married doesn't mean the kids won't have,
A very special feeling for both their mom and dad.

It's really quite important that the children realize.
Divorce just ends the marriage, we'll still be in their lives.

Don't Cry for Me

Don't cry for me, my children, because my life is gone

For just because I'm dying will not mean you are alone

God has always been my strength, on Him you can depend

You will not ever be alone, He'll be there till the end

When my life is ended and I am heaven bound

My troubles will be over and peace I will have found

There won't be any reason for you to cry for me

The tears you will be crying will fall for your own needs

For all of us die someday, I thank God that it is so

When wearied of the battle we can claim the joy that's owed

Lost Love

Two years ago next month we met
I doubt that I shall 'ere forget
The twinkle in his big brown eyes
For happiness inside them lies
He laughed a lot, he joked and cheered
For everything had humor near

I wonder if I love him still
I wonder if I really feel
A love inside for him today
I wish that it would go away
Forget the happiness I knew
So I could start my life anew

Maybe just remember it yet
As something I should not forget
As moments of the sweetest kind
As cherished memories sublime
Sort out, if I miss him still
Or just the way he made me feel

Why do we quickly stash away
The hurts that were in every day
To wish and long for "might have been"
Spend so much time remembering when
The choice is ours to love again
Or lose our life remembering when

The Quick Tongue of a Fool

Why do so many people say things that they don't mean?

Verbally hurting each other, it's a mystery to me.

My grandmother was like that, her words cut me to shreds.

Told me that I'd miss her, some day when she was dead.

The only thing I knew then was that I doubted it,

Often I would wonder why she'd cut me to the quick.

She told me I was the stupidest thing that God ever let live.

And that He gave a goose more brains than He put in my head.

It took till I was thirty to get over the pain.

Thinking that I was an idiot, a girl without a brain.

A full-time job and college with raising two kids too,

I tried so much to measure up, show her how little she knew.

Then I burned myself out, I stopped to view my life.

Was I trying too hard to prove Grandma wasn't right?

All those years she cut me down, I never realized

Just how much I believed her, believed all her lies.

For God had surely given me enough brains for my needs.

Her foolish cuts against me hurt more than I could see.

There are a lot of people who speak before they think

I'm sure they don't realize how deep it really sinks.

Diet Help

You told me I shouldn't worry cause the little girl was fat.

"She takes after her daddy, the whole family looks like that."

Alone she sat all by herself while the other children played.

She looked so lost and miserable as I glanced over her way.

So many times we just assume she will get over it.

She'll play with others her own size, you told me she was fit.

But we should all be concerned about health care and her joy.

So many girls who can't compete hurt themselves to avoid.

They want so much to fit in, to become accepted, fit and slim.

So easy to overlook her pain as everyone fights to be trim.

I pray she'll find a way to deal with all the loneliness she hates.

I pray she'll find the answer, and lose weight, not isolate.

Loneliness and low self-esteem can make this world seem so mean.

Escape in drugs or pills for some, but others, suicide succumb.

Let's help her while we can and show her diet tricks.

Let's pray to God to bring her joy, and ways to trim her hips.

She Didn't Cry

The phone rang and they summoned her
And even while she stood
They told her that her father died
She said she understood

They asked if she would inform
The rest of the family
She set about the process
Yet never showed her grief

She called her sister's family
She told the husband first
The other sister's husband too
It all seemed so rehearsed

Then even though others could've
It seemed she would insist
She told her mother of the shot
And how her dad was hit

She was a rock for everyone
Took care of each detail
Through the intervening days
She never stopped to wail

Then months passed, she hadn't cried
Yet her life seemed to change
From job to job she hopped along
As if she had been chased

Intellectually she had dealt
With her daddy's death
Emotionally she ran from it
Her life became a mess

Instead of dealing with her grief
She ran from it each time
Never facing up to the hurt
That was etching her insides

She'd never actualized the loss
Never let emotions show
She denied herself therapeutic grief
By not letting the teardrops flow

She had waited too long
To escape from it all
It would have been better
Had she just sat down and bawled

Someone Who Likes Who I Am

You say that you love me yet you treat me so bad.

You seem to delight, dear, in making me sad.

Please hold all your comments I don't want to hear.

"It is for your own good" comes off sounding quite queer.

You say that you love me then in the same breath

You're telling me nicely to go starve to death.

You say I'm not thin enough and my hairdo must go

I should go change my dress and my makeup should show.

Life's so full of hate, dear, and troubles will come.

I don't need you near me when you are so glum.

We're not helping each other feel better and so

I think it'd be kinder if we parted, please go.

It was nice on occasions but they are far between

If only you could learn to stop being so mean.

We're kidding each other, it's not working out.

What your words aren't saying, your actions do shout.

Good-bye, love, the heartbreak will hurt for a while.

I shall soon recover then I'll learn to smile.

The world's full of others, you're one fish in the pan.

I'll go find me someone who likes who I am.

Were You There?

Were you there when I was growing up and felt the pains I felt?

    Did you have to take the verbal blows to your dignity that I'd been dealt?

Were the threads of your self-confidence mere whips of what they should?

    Did you wonder as a little child "was there anything I did good"?

Were you told that you weren't worth the power needed to blow you to hell?

    Was there someone you lived with who made you feel that well?

If you didn't feel that way about yourself when you were young,

    Then don't tell me I shouldn't have done anything I may have done!

Words

Every day I love you more than I did the day before

I just can't believe it's true that I keep on loving you

Don't you know the words you say are not inclined to go away?

They have a way of coming back something like a sneak attack

Though I love you very much and long to feel your tender touch

It hurts me so, you'll never know the sting inside the words you throw

I've heard it said that words can bleed and only children have the need

To throw their careless words around hurting any victim found

The saddest part is what they do, words build a wall between me and you

Unless God helps us tear it down, that wall will grow by leaps and bounds

Youth Regained?

I think there is a folly in the thought
That you would like to live your life again

I know I wouldn't want to have refought
The battles I've once won, I look ahead

My age gives me the wisdom of my view
I've felt so many hurts they carved my soul

They've made me understand the things I do
And aided in my quest to reach my goals

To have my youth again for its own sake
Would merely leave accomplished fights a fake

To keep the wisdom and go back again
Would bore me to a frazzle in the end

For God has placed the trials in my path
So I would know I've only but to ask

And He will give me courage for the climb
As I become the person He designed

Tears

Tears, tears, tears, tears, seems I've cried so many tears
I can't stop them from falling, I've held them back for years
When I think of life with you, seems all I do is cry
I've had so many heartbreaks, the years just pass me by
The kids are grown so we're alone, I don't know what to do
I just know I can't stand the thought of growing old with you
Thoughts of our growing old together bring on so many fears
How can I go on this way when thinking brings on tears?
The little disappointments and hurts that are so old
Have hidden themselves inside me, these thoughts I've never told
If we're to go on together and save these married years
You've got to help me get some help to conquer all my tears
I've got to pray that God will help and show me to forgive
For I alone have held these hurts the many years we've live
Your quietness and all the times you never are at home
Show me you have a few reserved feelings of your own
So if we're going to clear the air, a decision we must make
A counselor and the Lord must help for our marriage's sake
We need to talk, we have forgot, the closeness we once knew
Something soon must be done or I can't live with you

An Old Man

Please someone won't you listen

       As the old man cries for help

Is it just that you're too busy

       Preoccupied with yourself

In his ranting he is crying

       At the closing of his life

He wants only to be cared for

       Live in peace without strife

Though he can't take care of his life

       He still wants to control it

So he bellows at his loved ones

       And he cusses his wife a bit

He refrains from even trying

       For he's got no will to give

He's only striking out at life

       Afraid that he won't live

THOUGHTS

A Merry-Go-Round of Misery

I really do not understand why people are so mean
I saw a mother screaming as she drove along the street
She yelled and screamed and even though her windows were all closed
I could tell as her car propelled and wandered off the road
You couldn't see the little boy she yelled at by her side
Not until I passed her could I see him trying to hide
I got so mad to see her yell I wondered what to do
She reminded me of the boss I had, he treated me like that too
Yes I was forced to take that kind of treatment and abuse
The man who signed my paychecks screamed so profuse
That helpless little boy was not as fortunate as I
I could choose to quit my job when verbal blows would fly
Now who is out there fighting for children in verbal pain?
Who will patch his dignity when verbal blows begin again?
Only God can help that mother see the damage that she does
Only God can understand her hurts and know what is the cause
Maybe she has a boss like mine who murders her dignity
Maybe she doesn't realize it's hurting her family
Maybe she can't take her anger out on someone her own size
Maybe she doesn't understand what's eating her up inside
The car swerving back and forth she almost lost control
She could have killed them both that day and no one would have known

If people don't stop hurting and show kindness to those they meet
It's a merry-go-round of misery, it grows as people take a seat
The businessman yells at the businessman who missed a delivery date
Everyone wants to make the buck, no one can afford to wait
The employer yells at the employee, after all he is the boss,
The employee fumes as he rides home, anger builds with each road he'll cross
At home he takes it out on his wife, who too could've got it at work
So on down the line to the children till everyone's pride is hurt
Only if someone kicks the dog will the chain of events ever quit
The dog has the best reaction, for the kicker will get bit
So builds the daily frustration as the circle keeps spinning around
Someone with a gun and no wife to hit goes shooting off some rounds
People who've lost their patience with a world that beats them down
They go out on the street to get even, will society pay for this round?
If only we could spread kindness with the ease we spread hate and harm
This would become a better world with a little more love and charm
I quit my job and told my boss he couldn't treat me like a dog
I've heard he has been a lot nicer to the next girl who got the job
That was the way I was going to change the corner of the world that was mine
Maybe if other people would try we could clear up some stress in our time
With God's help I have found a job where I'm treated with respect
With God's help I've also learned how to give back the respect I get

Decisions

I ask of no one to approve of what I do,

I offer no explanation to any for what I've done.

I alone will understand, no one truly understands another.

I do know this my love, for me there is no other.

I've looked for love for many years,

A part of me has searched since I was born.

For not until we met and knew each other,

Did the missing half of me join the other.

Since I've found you I'll search for love no more.

Each day a joy comes that outshadows the day before.

Though this love of ours will stand the test of time,

What's to become of your wife and that husband of mine?

Bye

The people pleaser in me has to run away

> From the controller in you in order to find my way

The anger inside grows into negativity and depression

> Expressing itself in road rage and aggression

Before I understood this I got divorced, quit jobs, and ran from relationships. There are three personality types in us all: the controller, the pleaser, and the avoider. We have more of one type than another depending on which type worked best growing up. We can do all of these in different situations especially if we recognize what we are doing and how it is working for us. I found running away in order to get my needs met was my fallback cure. Recently I found myself in a relationship with another pleaser and saw how well it worked for me.

Clouds

Years ago I saw them not, nor did I notice birds a lot.

Sky and trees did not appear, I could not see beyond the tears.

When my hurt and anger passed, I noticed God's beauty at long last.

I noticed how green trees could be, I ceased to fear the bumblebee.

When I'm with God and clouds He made, I find life's problems seem to fade.

Grey and silver, white and black, all these colors looking back.

As I gaze in the heavens above, watching all the clouds I love.

Bright or dark clouds seem so free, free as a bird and light as a breeze.

Light and fluffy, whipped cream clean, clouds seem friendly, never mean.

Now with God I soon forget all the problems that made me fret.

Peace

The snowcapped hill looks down upon

A sleepy valley as morning dawns

And as a brook keeps up its pace

I feel I'm looking at God's face

Love

If you have never loved a love that has no end

That you would give your life for

You have never loved, my friend

Mountain Man

A voice as soft as wind itself and eyes a misty blue

    He stopped beside me on the trail and soon enough I knew

I wanted a chance to know this man who stood talking to me

    For wise he was and gentle too, so nice he seemed to be

The stars were close and bright above, he talked of many things

    So interesting and smart he was, a bottle of wine he did bring

We talked all night gazing at the moon and every star in the sky

    I'd never dreamed on a camping trip I could meet such a wonderful guy

Back in town at the office, his virtues seemed to grow

    Next weekend I rushed to the mountains, there was something I had to know

Would his eyes dance and make me laugh again as they did before

    Or was it just another world I invented to escape being bored?

Sunscreen

I put the sunscreen in the swimsuit drawer

So I will not forget it anymore

The pain I feel upon my chest and back

Soon fades away and I forget to pack

The sunscreen when I go out to play

My skin may not forgive me one fine day

Tidbits

I've heard you're going on a trip
Here's something you should know

When it comes to airplane travel
The luggage moves awfully slow

Through airport terminals I run
A pace so hard to keep

I wonder as the baggage comes
If I could get some sleep

* * * **

Father in Heaven, please help me I pray
My bank account gets smaller each day

I tithe a tenth of my income to you
Show me your wisdom to make the rest due

* * * **

When morning fills the sky
Till evening shadows fall

I find between these two events
The greatest joys of all

Picking up the Pieces

There is a void that must be filled

When love has gone away

It's filled with hope and faith to know

New love will come your way.

Think Thin

I really need to lose some weight, my size I have begun to hate

For when I tip the scale each day. Boy do I feel fat!

When I was young, how I could eat, "a hollow leg" was said of me

But since I had my two babies, boy did I get fat!

It's not that I eat lots of sweets, oh once in a while I sneak a treat

I just get bored and so I eat. Boy do I feel fat!

Those mental tricks I try to play, as if I think it will go away

When I get dressed it makes me say, "Boy do I look fat!"

The guiltier I seem to feel, the larger I find I make the meal

This merry-go-round is never still. I'm going to stay fat?

This gluttony must be a sin, I have to see myself as thin

Pray that God will help me win my battle against fat!

I know I can't do it alone. God must help me with my goal

Discipline and patience I will know. I will lose my fat!

Take Five

Ever see a camper trailer and wish you were inside
    Knowing that in the morning you were going for a ride?

Long to throw your fishing pole into a mountain stream
    To walk along a river, capture a beautiful scene?

Long to wake at sunup in a tent by the riverside,
    Breathe the smell of pine trees and watch water flow by?

Long to find the stillness of listening to the breeze,
    Rest beside a rippling brook to put your nerves at ease?

It's hard to find these moments of precious solitude
    When you're fighting the morning traffic, many people being rude.

One morning as I drove to work I looked up at the sky
    Amidst the solid blue above white fluffy clouds went by.

I pulled my car off the road and gazed up at the clouds.
    I took an extra minute to retreat from all the crowds.

I sat quietly and watched them as they softly fluffed on by,
    It seemed just then I realized I could find peace if I tried.

The next day I left early and stopped in the same lot,
    I'd brought along a thermos to my heavenly viewing spot.

I stopped to smell the roses as the songs so aptly say
    You can find a lot of reasons to be happy for each day.

Now I take an extra moment to find quiet in my life
    It's far better than tranquilizers to take away my strife.

If the only vacations I get are the five-minute ones I take
    It's far better than constant worry and more useful than coffee breaks.

A leisurely drive in the morning has a tranquil effect on the day
    Five minutes of calm meditation brings deep reassurance my way

They're more precious than hectic vacations and I can "take five" every day.
    There are so many people all strung out, complaining is all they can say.

I find that my time can be better spent relaxing in mental escapes.
    "Take five" whenever I need it and visualize a peaceful landscape.

As the office reaches a feverish pace and I really wish I could quit.
    I "take five" and see cool clear water, it refreshes my spirit a bit.

I can take a calm look at the problem and not be too hasty to act.
    In the stillness I gain a perspective and I find a new line of attack.

I "take five" before I start yelling, I "take five" before I explode.
    I "take five" and recapture my patience and take the situation in hold!

Free Will

He was deaf and so dependent on me

    He seemed so helpless due to his disability

A real homebody never wanting to roam

    He'd always be there waiting when I'd come home

As the months passed, I knew I liked having him around

    He was so loyal, a quality not usually found

Yet as the days passed and they turned into months

    I was so worried 'cause I loved him so much

I went with him to an ear doctor I knew

    To see if somehow there was something they could do

An operation it wasn't so hard

    There was a chance the damage to retard

Now I worried if this worked would he be gone

    If I had a right to hold him back, would it be wrong?

If he was fixed up, would he up and go away?

    What right had I to hold him back if he didn't want to stay?

If you love someone and they truly want to leave

    Can you force them? Wouldn't they leave eventually?

It was his life, he didn't owe me a thing

    He had the treatment, he could now hear everything

I won also for he didn't go away

    Soon I knew he loved me and would never stray

I'm oh so very happy for his company

    My stray cat loves me, it will always be that way

My Soul Longs for the Seasons of My Youth

To see it snow again upon my window pane

    To watch the snow as it melts into rain

Inside me there's a hunger I can't soothe

    My soul longs for the seasons of my youth

To see the ground thaw out in early spring

    To listen to the birds their greetings bring

To come alive to times of hope and truth

    My soul longs for the seasons of my youth

When summer comes and fishing poles men throw

    To listen to the joyful games and row

Float dreamily recalling old love tunes

    My soul longs for the seasons of my youth

Where reds and yellows colored up my life

    As dying leaves gave up without a fight

Where careless hours were something I could lose

    My soul longs for the seasons of my youth

Oh Lord, Won't You Bring Me!

Oh Lord, won't you bring me some positivity?
    This stupid virus is trying to scare me.

I never hear a word about anything good you see.
    Oh Lord, won't you bring me some positivity?

Oh Lord, am I losing what's left of my brain?
    This constant local crisis is driving me insane.

I cannot remember anything that makes me glad.
    Oh Lord, I'm so tired of feeling so bad!

Oh Lord, won't you send me a message today?
    One that will help me drive this gloom away.

Oh Lord, you're so good and so wonderful to me.
    Oh Lord, won't you send up some positivity!

Why Did I Buy the Air Fryer?

I saw it on a TV set while eating with my friends
So simple and so easy it went right to my head

I hate to cook and what's this, for it had so many parts
I should have watched more YouTube, seeing others before I start

Watch some YouTube videos before you purchase one
Unfortunately I did that after the deed was done

On TV the guy was convincing of how easy the things were to make
On some of the YouTube videos, the purchase was such a mistake

Now I have so many parts I won't use and no place to store the thing
Thinking about an air fryer? Oh, please just think again

Now what do I do with the packing, so much to take to the trash
Lessons I learned after the fact, that's why this place is distressed

Wait, there on YouTube, "John Eats Cheap" was playing
40-minute baked potatoes, a mouthwatering creation!

When the Quarantine Is Over

I'm going to buy some green paint and paint the bedroom wall.

I'm going to order a toilet and change the bathroom stall.

I'm going to have a big dinner and see my family again.

I'm going to see my girlfriends. Oh Lord, how long it's been.

I'm going to go out to eat each Monday like I used to.

My husband will go see the boys on Wednesday mornings too.

I'll go out to the bookstore and buy some books to read.

I'll go to the mall and walk around exercising my knees.

I'll give up cleaning the house and go to the store and spend.

I'll be glad we're all heathy, back to normal life again.

GROWTH

Forbidden Fruit

There is nothing so appealing as what you cannot have,
    Just knowing that you want it, the desire becomes so bad.
She loved him very much and yet maybe his wife did too,
    He must have had a good laugh at the tortures she went through.

They fell in love so suddenly, it never should have been,
    It happened just by accident, the closeness of two friends.
So easy to talk to each other, so nice to be around,
    Soon it was more than closeness, love grew by leaps and bounds.

When she learned he was married, she told him she must leave.
    It was so hard to let him go, for days she cried and grieved.
He sent her lovely roses and begged her to come back.
    Her head said she must stay away, her heart denied the fact.

For never had she loved someone who possessed her heart and soul.
    Even though her head said go away, her heart wouldn't let him go.
He made it seem like heaven on earth when she was in his arms.
    He made her feel so pretty, resolve melted from his charm.

So on and on this love affair kept burning out their lives.
    As they got more attached it seemed, fear grew before his eyes.
Two months had passed since she had said they would have to part.
    When he anguished to tell her that his wife still had his heart.

He had led her on, believing that his marriage was soon through,
    A glimpse of his devotion to his wife came from out of the blue.
So she told him again it was over as there was no future for her,
    Yet he begged her to not go away, her absence he couldn't endure.

There is something so enchanting about what you shouldn't do.
    It seems that it'll possess you, that without it you are through.
She loved him so and it thrilled her just to hear his sexy voice.
    Yet alarmed her, as it seemed to her, she no longer had a choice.

So she went away on vacation, to just think for awhile.
    To the mountains she'd go fishing and try to forget his smile.
But he followed her to the mountains, he found her in the hills.
    She loved him now more than before, he possessed her every will.

Two more months went by since the last good-bye, things had grown to a fever pitch.
    So he told his wife about them, expecting her to pitch a fit.
Things had gotten so complicated and he didn't know how to cope.
    His wife told him to end it if their marriage had any hope.

Though she couldn't deal with the turnaround, it was peaceful they were through.
    She was so tired of sneaking around, a new future to look forward to.
She could build a life of her own somehow, but little did she know.
    He came back again in two months and said he just couldn't let her go.

This seemed so strange for he wasn't free, what could he expect her to do?
    Seems he wanted a good-time lady, so she told him they were through.
As you may expect he came back again in two months like before.
    Said that his wife was leaving, now this opened up a new door.

Forbidden fruit is so tasty, till you've taken a good bite.
    Now when these lovers get together would you think that they would fight?
It wasn't too long and it ended, they both were agreed upon it.
    It had lasted two months till they parted and had hurt one another a bit.

Seems that something you want is so thrilling when it isn't within your reach.
    It seems to have thorns aplenty and a very good lessen to teach.
Soon you see that no one is perfect, it is something you didn't want to see.
    Could she accept him with complications, not at all what he seemed to be?

When you can't have a job or someone that you set your heart on to own,
    You never believe in the notion, you wouldn't want it if its true self were shown.
To lose his home was a gamble, he had driven his wife out the door.
    He couldn't get back all the trust she had, but his wife took him back once more.

Choose

Why do you criticize me in front of our son
　　Pointing out things you think I have done.

I'm a good driver, no tickets, no fines
　　Yet when I'm driving, your comments deride.

I've never had a ticket, I'm solid it's true
　　I pay all my debts, work hard, so do you.

We've so much between us to show him the way
　　We need to remember the good in each day.

To focus on all that we've done through the years
　　To build us a future with hope and not fear.

Let's give ourselves credit and praise every day
　　We're both working hard, let's show him the way.

Encourage each other, point out our success
　　Build on the good things, encourage his best.

Our world is so negative if you listen to the news
　　Let's not let that into our home, Let's choose

Choose to be happy and choose to be glad
Point out our blessings and the love what we have!

Marriage is a compromise at times. What feels like criticism is the other person expressing his worry about his wife and child.

If Only

"If only" is a cop-out phrase and causes many pains
It offers you an alibi or roadblock in the way
You'll never learn to live your life in the present times
If you're always thinking back on days you left behind

"If only" just reminds me of a cowboy I once knew
How he let "if only" ruin all the things he'd do
"If only" as a child he hadn't jumped up on that bronc
Wrapped the rope around his thumb trying to hang on

"If only" he'd have realized he was to lose his thumb
"If only" he keeps saying, can it change the things he's done?
"If only" he had married someone else, he will say
Maybe he'd have been someplace else on that fateful day

"If only" she'd been true to him he wouldn't have been shot
By the man he found her with, "if only" is all he's got
Bullets don't go back inside of gun barrels you see
"If only" will not erase his pain and misery

"If only" he could stop himself from bitter reminiscence
He could have tried to live with it and kept his children with him
"If only" he kept consuming all his time and his concern
Making him a bitter man, I hope someday he'll learn

His disability remains from that fateful night
It isn't his wheelchair that drives people from his sight
It's his bitter looking back at things that could have been
"If only" is his escape from a life that could be lived

There are a lot of people who are crippled and paralyzed
They refuse to accept defeat and give up on their lives
They do not waste the hours on "if only" wasted dreams
They concentrate on visions and see life within their means

They see themselves as being something better than before
They see this limitation as a challenge opening doors
They realize that sometimes you can do more on two wheels
Than others do on two feet, it's the challenges they feel

The future always offers what your visions show to you
You can make things happen just believe in what you do
There're so many possibilities if we'd take the time to dream
God will show us how to face opportunities that we see

With positive assurance we can conquer all life's blows
Making something of our life, it's up to us you know
So give up your "if only," don't just sit there wondering why
In every disadvantage, you'll find advantages if you try

Don't think about "if only," the best is yet to be
Just think about the future, there is nothing you can't be

It's Your Mood, Control It!

You can decide the way you'll feel on any given day.
You must believe that everything is going to go your way.

You cannot find your happiness, that's something you must make.
Look for the good in everything, think positive for your sake.

Create a mental climate that fosters growth of mind.
Happy, positive attitudes, leave gloominess behind.

While those around you look so sad soon making others glum.
Remember you can change it, you are the only one.

In David D. Burns's book *Feeling Good*, he states:
Feelings are not facts; you can change your feelings by changing your thinking.
It's not events that determine your state of mind, but how you feel about the event.
Learn to challenge your own thoughts, look at your accomplishments and begin to feel good!
Depression is not an emotional disorder, bad feelings we have in depression all stem from
negative thoughts. Therefore the treatment must be about challenging those thoughts. (pages
28–29)

In Martin E. P. Seligman's book *Authentic Happiness*:
Emotions are generated by cognition: Thoughts of danger cause anxiety, thoughts of loss
cause sadness, thoughts of trespass cause anger, your train of thought leads to your mood.
Thoughts of depressed people are dominated by negative interpretations of the past, of the

future, and of their abilities. Learning to argue against these pessimistic interpretations of themselves relieves depression to about the same extent as antidepressant drugs (with less relapse and recurrence). (pages 64–65)

Raising children is about identifying and amplifying their strengths and virtues, and helping them find the niche where they can live these positive traits to the fullest. (pages 28–29)

Twentieth Class Reunion

So long ago it seems to me that day we first did meet.

Your curly hair, your gentle hand, a voice so soft and sweet.

Though many years have gone between there's something concrete left.

Good memories of a tender crush, one that I'll not forget.

Many hurts and disappointments, men have cut me to the quick.

So many times a handsome man has hurt and made me sick.

Though twenty years of time have past I look back and cherish you.

Shining in my past somewhere a friend so tried and true.

You treated me like a lady, you held me high apart.

I hope it was because I had a special place in your heart.

Put Yourself in His Place

Have you ever thought too much about the other guy?
    When someone did a stupid thing, did you wonder why?

A teenage boy had pulled in front of traffic moving slow.
    Squeezed his truck in silly so no one had room to go.

Resulting in a traffic jam at the grocery store parking lot.
    An old man had to pull back into his parking spot.

A younger man was so irate, his language you would not repeat.
    Called the boy some names that would have knocked you off your seat.

They both were mad, it made you sad for no one realized
    Experience is a teacher, for in it much wisdom lies.

The boy had learned a lesson and he wouldn't do that again.
    I know because I sat in the truck right next to him.

I'm sure the other people went off fuming from the spot.
    If they had made a traffic error, I'll bet they long forgot.

Their day could have been brighter if they'd taken time to think,
    How bad that boy must have felt, next time he'd have to think.

He sat there looking silly, all he could do was grin,
 Hoping no one he knew had seen him blunder in.

If that old man had laughed it off, instead he took offense.
 Quite positive it was a jab at his age and circumstance.

The other man could have reminisced about his younger days.
 For with his nasty temper, he must have made some waves.

The only one with humor was the unlearned teenage youth.
 For from this sharp experience, he learned a thing or two.

He learned he should look ahead when traffic's moving slow.
 He learned to be more patient when the other guy's ignorance shows.

He learned he'd get there sooner if he'd only use his head.
 I know 'cause as I sat there on the way home, his face was red.

Inheritance Now?

No matter how much you love someone who's leaving you the funds
When you need the money, would you wish their death would come?
Would you leave them more money if they were nice to you?
Is the will all sealed and final? Is there nothing you can do?

You can see their eyes widen as you enter the hospital door.
This is it, they would mutter, what'll they spend their money for?
Did they think of all the many years when you were by their side?
Did they think of how you held them when they hurt deep down inside?

Did they remember years ago when you would lend them funds?
How their kids would have gone hungry, how much the money's done?
Do they think about your comfort in these your dying days?
Did they all come 'round to help you? Did they try in any way?

As they mutter how it can't be long before the hour comes.
When you got better, did they rejoice? Or did it sadden some?
Isn't there just a little part in everybody's soul,
That thinks of the inheritance before the rich ones go?

If we could only channel our concern in other ways
Give comfort to the aging, help them face their dying days.
A little care would brighten up the corner where they lie.
Remembering we will be there, who knows how soon we'll die.

Why not provide while you're alive and watch the fun they have
You'd be around to guide them from choices that are bad.
You could provide them in a way that showed what they could do,
And when you're gone they'd miss the friend who made their dreams come true.

No Good Looking Back

Love is a very special thing that so few people share.

    The thrill of someone special, the magic in the air.

I loved him once so long ago; my heart had learned to sing.

    With him a cup of coffee was a very special thing.

That was then and this is now, oh, tell me is it gone?

    I wonder if this feeling was meant to linger on.

At times I'd give my earthly wealth for just one night with him.

    But even if I did go back, the feeling wouldn't begin.

I couldn't touch the love I felt for time took that away.

    There is no good in looking back, I'd just waste my today.

Not That Hard to Love

You held me in your confidence and showed me how to live
You hold me at a distance now, your love you cannot give
You held me close and whispered how you wanted to be with me
A distance is between us now, only time can set that free

I don't intend to wait till then or for your love I'll fight
I want someone who'll care for me not just when I look right.
I want someone who'll love me whether I am fat or thin.
Someone who'll love me when I'm sick and nothing makes me grin.

It doesn't matter how I look, he'll love me any way.
I want someone to love me even when I am away
I don't want to have to worry if I look good enough for you
If you don't love me all the time, your love will never do.

How could it stand the strain of life when troubles come our way?
We must love each other all the time to make it through each day
I know I'm not that hard to love so if it's hard for you
Then it just means you're not the one. I'm sure that you won't do.

I may not be a beauty like you see each night on TV
Even if I were ugly, there's someone out there for me
So if you think I'll apologize because I don't suit you
Well, buddy, you can think again! Find another, we are through!

About That Job

They told me I was crazy when I said I had to leave.
　　I told them it didn't matter, that it was up to me.

God gave me a calling and I knew I had to go.
　　I couldn't disappoint Him because I loved Him so.

It started on an April day, I was picnicking in the woods.
　　My friend said, "You are crazy, do you really think you should?"

"You're making so much money, you can't get that again."
　　"Money isn't everything, I'm not happy there," I said.

I'm over my head in that office, I'm underqualified.
　　It's just like the Peter Principle, the book I read described.

It's my level of incompetence, it's not working out at all.
　　I'd rather leave right now than to take a nasty fall.

I struggle all the time I'm here, and worry they'll find out.
　　That I'm not sure of what I do, goof up and get kicked out.

I'm selling all that I possess and moving out of town.
　　God's telling me what I should do. He'll never let me down.

God loves me. I'm His child, you know, and He'll take care of me.
    Some distant destination is where I long to be.

I'm leaving in June to find a job, in Oracle, a country town.
    If that's not where I belong, God will guide me around.

Those waiting months were dreadful, my employer was surprised.
    Embarrassed that I wasn't qualified, for he never realized.

I gave them two months' notice, it seemed such a very long time.
    I just couldn't wait to get going, to the place God had in mind.

I took awhile after that job, to go camping and relax.
    Everyone said, "You're crazy, soon you'll be going back."

In my thirty years of living, I'd worked at least fifteen.
    There was another side of my life, God now was showing me.

I'd thought I was a career girl, I'd always wanted to work.
    I began to realize how much I enjoyed housework.

After I learned that lesson, I felt it was time to be employed.
    I'd exhausted the little town's options, I sought a job I enjoyed.

I had bills to pay and two kids to be fed.
    I moved my trailer down to Tucson instead.

My funds were running low, but I knew God would see me through.
    God showed me where to go to get a résumé that would do.

I knew I wouldn't get a reference from the last two jobs I had.
    The employment office told me the prospects in town were bad.

I left it up to God then, that a job would come my way.
    After only six interviews at places, I wouldn't want to stay.

I got a crazy phone call from a couple in interior design.
    After only one interview, it was clear it was a great job to find.

God is great and God is good, and it was in two weeks' time.
    I got that job, it paid well, and it was in the perfect time.

I got that job on Tuesday, I moved my trailer down on Thursday.
    The kids started school on Monday, and it all worked out in God's way.

It was about a year later when I had the urge to quit.
    I told them I was leaving, they thought I was an idiot.

I had started there in August, I had gone through so many things.
    There'd been so many trials there, I'd learned so many things.

I learned to handle their tempers, the insults I put up with a lot.
    I learned a lesson in patience and the power of positive thought.

God showed me wisdom that can be found in sticking to your guns.
Wanting something bad enough had power to make it come.

I'd learned a lot about myself and how many people get by.
No matter what the problem is, it'll work out if you try.

I had received an offer for a management position.
I hadn't applied for it, so I knew it was God's decision.

Though I had to take a cut in pay, I really didn't mind.
I couldn't advance where I was at, I had new horizons in mind.

Both times I'd quit the job I had because I couldn't see,
Why people stay in positions where they just aren't meant to be.

The first job had been so bad because I was undertrained.
That was the worst feeling I had, the insecurity that I faced.

I'm sure there are many people who just keep hanging on.
Even though every morning they just wish the job was gone.

Trusting in God to guide you will raise those burdens up.
God will work beside you. He can fill your living cup.

He'll show you when it's time to leave or if you just must stay.
If you're to stay and learn from it or leave and find your way.

Trusting God to guide me, I'm going to do better you'll see.
    Closer to that sought-for dream, God's put His peace in me.

It doesn't matter if people think you're crazy, how can they know?
    They like the security of their desk and watch their enthusiasm go.

So many lives are wasted, brains shifted into low gear.
    People are afraid to change and better their careers.

Well I've got guts and at thirty-three, I'm still trusting in the Lord.
    I know I'm on the threshold, great adventure is in store.

Staying Single

Momma, you don't understand how hard it is these days.
    You need to date someone today to understand our ways.

I tell you, Mom, it's very hard a decent man to find.
    You try so hard each date you have to keep an open mind.

Time after time you realize so many want one thing.
    Fight after fight you soon give up and toss love in the ring.

It's so much easier, Momma, my own company to keep.
    Much easier to live alone and tend to my own needs.

I'd rather live my own life and keep just to myself.
    I'll put my dreams of marriage back high upon the shelf.

Momma, you may be upset your expectations I can't keep.
    Remember, Mom, it is my life, and my needs I must meet.

I've had a lot of time to think and I have realized.
    God may have some other thoughts about my future life.

When I was so very lonesome and feeling oh so blue.
    I found God there, I know He cares, His love will see me through.

I know He'll always be my friend and that He cares for me.
    He loves me more than anyone, His love will shelter me.

I'll just grow closer to Him, growing in faith and love.
    Knowing that I'll never be lonely, I have a great love from above.

So Momma, don't you worry if single I choose to be.
    God is my guide, He's by my side, and He'll look after me.

Brand New Start

There are in life no guarantees that he will always care for thee
Only time will let you know if he will stay or if he'll go
Worrying won't change his mind, remember another you can find
Don't hold on to the hurts you feel that slow your heart so it won't heal
Just hang onto those memories that made you feel so darn pretty
Remember there will someday be another one who will love thee
For none of us can really see if what we want is what we need
We sit around and lick our wounds crying over old love tunes
Instead of looking gleefully on a new horizon for us to see
Tomorrow brings a new romance, smile and give it half a chance
Tomorrow brings a sunny day, tonight's tears will fade away
Somebody else was meant for you, remember half a love won't do
You want someone who wants you too, somebody who would not hurt you
Someone who loves your every mood who loves your laugh and giggle too
To love you whether fat or thin, who only wants you to want them
Who'll make you feel a joy each day you'll know they'll never go away
While basking in this brilliant love, you'll know the joy love is made of
Only when you're loved that way should you plan a wedding day
You'll look back on this broken heart, you'll see if was a brand new start

The Mistake

How can you forgive me for what I've done to you?

Can I hide behind the fact that I was just a youth?

I was only sixteen when I stole your beau away.

I didn't like the one I had, so I took yours that day.

I rationalize that if he'd leave, he must not have cared for you.

Yet how was I to understand I ruined our friendship too?

Years have passed and I forgot his name so long ago.

I will not forget how close we were, I really miss you so.

I didn't learn my lesson for oh so many years.

Thinking back on how it was, missing you brings tears.

Tears, I'm sure you must have cried, when I did that to you.

I kick myself for my mistake but that alone won't do.

I just have to tell you I'm sorry and so sad.

I miss you cousin dearly, and I feel so very bad.

Abortion

Choose, choose, choose, choose my insides seemed to say
Should I have this baby or is abortion the only way?
I wondered as I sat upon the moving merry-go-round
Should I have this baby when the father's not around?

Around, around, around it went, it matched my inner state
Should I run the gamut? Do I know what is at stake?
Abortion seems an awful thing and it conjures up some gloom
If I could take that option, I would have to do it soon

The year is 1969, the possibilities are few
To Mexico I'd have to go, my mood is very blue
Three years ago my roommate had done that very thing
Her experience and the tales she tells sure make that option sting

My grandmother is quite the prude, she told me what to do
"Adoption is the only way, my dear don't be a fool"
My mother says to have it after all I'm rather set
There are a lot of men who make less money than I get

It wasn't just the money, it's the responsibility

How could I care for someone else, I can't take care of me

Just then I saw two little boys playing on the swing

They were so cute and precious, it really made me think

Choose, choose, chooose, choose my insides say again

I wonder if this decision is made by many women?

There were too many variables just too much to decide

I had to have some insight, a view from the other side

"Lord help me make my mind up, I don't know what to do

I know there is no choice too large and You will see me through"

It didn't take too very long before the answer came

I knew I'd have the baby. God answered me that day.

An Unanswered Question

On afternoons I loved to dance alone upon the grass and stones
The lovely oaks would line the lane and follow where I'd go
It was a very pretty spot this cemetery fair
I loved to go for many walks, I felt so peaceful there

I often pondered on a name, I wondered how they lived
I seemed to feel they died in peace like the writings on them said
But do we know how often anybody dies in peace?
Isn't it more likely that ourselves we do deceive?

For unless somebody's perfect with two arms and two feet
Nobody seems to need them, nobody wants to see
It seems if we're not perfect, not macho, trim, or fit
Nobody seems to need you, they'd throw you in a ditch

Employers when they're looking are very quick to choose
No fatties and no oldies, even ugliness won't do
You see it starts at every age this feeling of uselessness
It seems you must be perfect to measure up in this mess

How many of the dying are shut off from the world?
They suffer with their feelings, deserted and disturbed
They long so to be useful to help the ones they love
But most of all they're longing so much just to be loved

In dying we want freedom from misery and pain
We need so to feel kindness and dignity again
We long for someone's caring and acceptance for who we are
To be groomed and attractive, though death is not that far

Our favorite food, some flowers, and music that will soothe
To be remembered kindly and think back on our youth
We give so much attention to athletes and stars
The older ones among us are deserted where they are

What we fail to understand is so soon we'll be there
For each of us is dying and no one seems to care
There's so much we could give others we only need to dare
Let's show them that we love them and we know that they are there

Feel Your Grief

Come visit me in the funeral home
Come visit the body I leave

Touch me so you'll know I'm gone
Realize it's my body not me

Like the cocoon that's left behind
As the butterfly breaks through to flight

I've left that set of bones behind
And my spirit can now take flight

No longer to stand with pains in my back
Now I can fly and dance

And never will I come back
Not even if I had the chance

Don't cry for me for I am free
I'll always watch after you

Come view my bones so you will know
I don't walk the world as you do

So cry my child and feel your grief
And let the feelings go

The sooner you hurt, the sooner relief
My love will stop the flow.

Lessons

A problem is a lesson that is sent from God above

Each problem has a reason they are tokens of God's love

God gives us strength to meet each one that comes along today

These exercises build our faith, God's with us all the way

Love Outgrown

After putting up with your vanity

        I'm losing all my sanity

I wish you'd leave and never call

        before you drive me up the wall

You know you have a way it seems

        Of blocking out the sunshine beams

In case my message you can't get

        Your face I'm trying to forget

I want to be as kind with tact

        Old love you'll have to face the fact

We'll have to say good-bye my friend

        I hope we will not meet again

Now that this speech I have rehearsed

        My shyness seems to be my curse

How do I say the words good-bye,

        When gazing into your blue eyes?

Goodbye

I cried myself to sleep that night you called to me on the phone.

   You asked me if I'd fix you up with one of the girls I've known.

Oh darling can't you understand that I love only you,

   And it would tear me up inside to see anyone with you.

I know that I don't own you, I have no claim that's true.

   Yet if we go on dating, there's one thing we must do.

We must discuss this thoroughly, I'm not sure you understand.

   It's oh so very important that you know just where I stand.

For I'm a one-man woman, I expect the same from you.

   So if you want to date my friend, I'm sure that we are through.

Resolve

You know when you resolve to live your life a different way

To straighten up your act somehow in a positive way

You know exactly why it didn't work out so well before

Everything will be different than it was, you are sure

Then pretty soon it all comes around the way it used to be

The problems are back and bigger, this time you quickly see

You brought the same old habits to the problem once again

Resolve to break those habits, that is how to win my friend

Wishing Won't Do

When I was just a little girl and you were twenty-one,
I would pretend that I was you, you were the pretty one.

You had the best of everything, your husband was so cute.
A beautiful house, three darling kids, I really looked up to you.

I remember you were tall and thin, the lovely clothes you used to wear.
I wanted to grow up just like you for years I wished I were there.

Now that I am all grown up, I've had a chance to learn,
Just how hard your life was and how maybe the table turned.

I now know your good-looking man chased women all over town.
How he'd get so nasty drunk and how he'd knock you around.

How jealous he'd been of your slenderness, how dreadful he'd been to you.
How hard it had been to leave him and give up your pretty house too.

So often things aren't as they seem and we shouldn't waste our time,
Dreaming of things that might have been, missing our own good times.

God says do not covet your neighbor's property.
Wanting the things you don't have won't make you very happy.

Want the things you do have, enjoy all the little things.
God will supply the things you need, a much happier life it'll bring.

Believe in Yourself

You've heard it said so often that the "rich get richer"
So how without money will you ever do better?
The only thing that separates the rich people from you
They know they're rich and they believe in everything they do
The only thought the rich allow to come into their head
Are positive assurances that they will get ahead
They have an overpowering belief they will succeed
If we believed as they did, there is nothing we couldn't be
There is a wondrous power in the thoughts you hold inside
In seeing yourself a winner, you have victory on your side
Some people say to get ahead you must have a degree
A lot of high executives spell worse than you and me
As long as you believe in you, there's nothing you can't be
God has a dream for us to be the best that we can be
So say a prayer to God above and see the victory won
Believe that you're a winner and it's already done